WHAT MACHINES DO AT WORK

Written by John Allan
Illustrated by Esther Cuadrado

First published in 2022 by Hungry Tomato Ltd
F1, Old Bakery Studios, Blewetts Wharf, Malpas Road, Truro, Cornwall, TR1 1QH, UK.

A CIP catalog record for this book is available from the British Library.

ISBN 978-1-914087-52-3

Manufactured in the USA

Discover more at
www.hungrytomato.com

CONTENTS

WHAT DO MACHINES DO AT WORK?

We use them for all sorts of tasks, from paving a road to milking a cow. Life would be much harder and less fun without them.

HARD AT WORK

Lots of us use machines to help us do our jobs every day. Some machines can build things or move stuff around. They can also fix things for us, and even save lives!

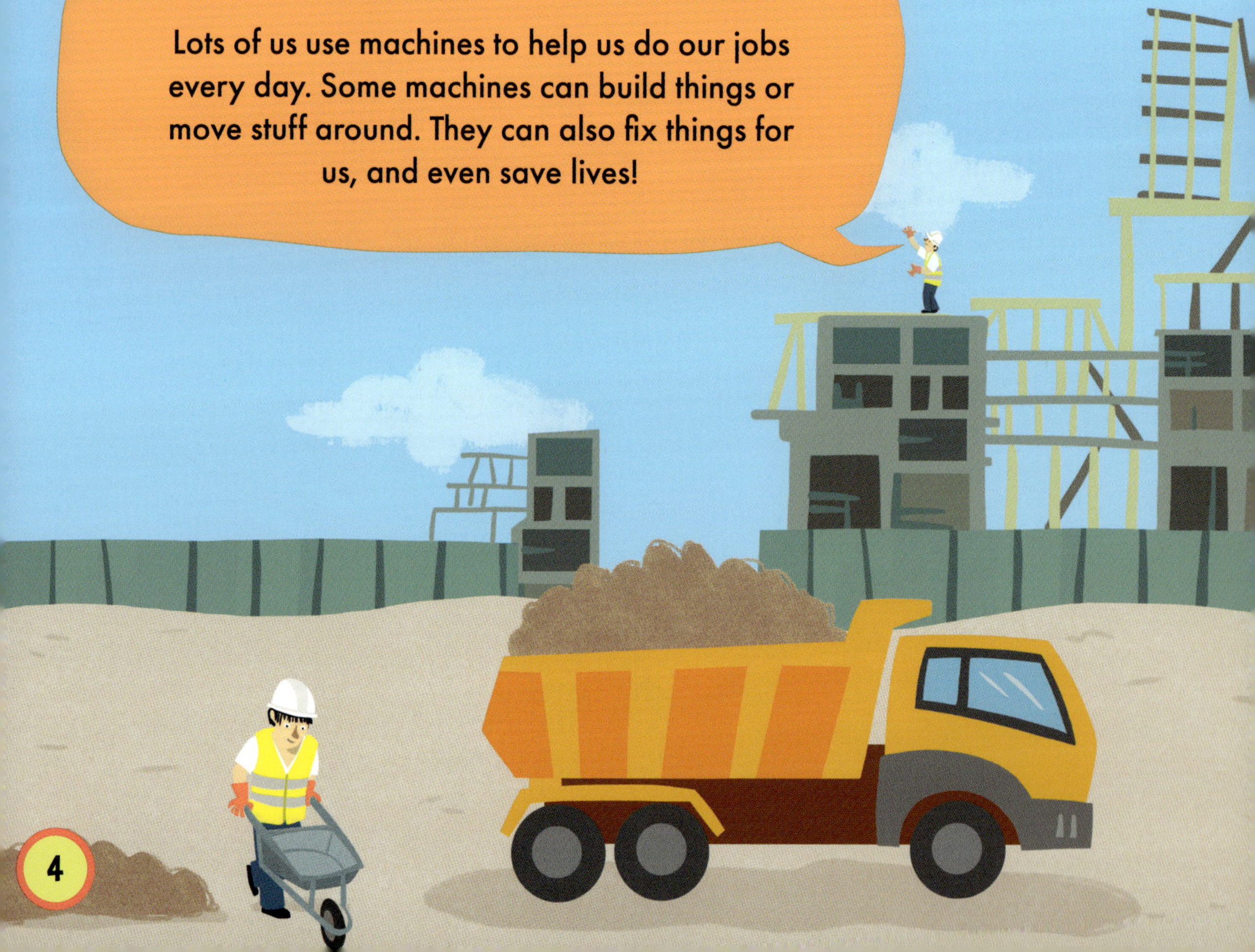

LET'S GET GOING!

Prepare to visit lots of busy machines at work. Take a look at them in action, then turn the page to discover what they do and how they work.

ON THE CONSTRUCTION SITE

There is a lot going on at this construction site. Look at the big, heavy machines helping the builders with their work.

STOP

ON THE CONSTRUCTION SITE

Bulldozers are used to clear the ground to get it ready for building.

Tracks help it move over muddy and uneven ground.

Bulldozer

Dump trucks are used to carry heavy loads of materials like sand, gravel or soil.

It can lift and tip its box to empty its load.

Dump Truck

Excavators are used to dig up soil from the ground.

This long **hydraulic** arm is called a boom.

Excavator

These machines are used to drill giant holes.

Hydraulic Drill

The drill twists into the ground like a corkscrew.

Very strong cables are used to raise and lower its load.

Crane

Cranes are used to lift large and heavy objects around the construction site.

This truck makes concrete by mixing sand, gravel, water and cement in its drum.

This drum turns round and round to mix the concrete.

Concrete Mixer

ON THE FARM

There's lots to do on the farm. Machines can make a farmer's job much easier.

ON THE FARM

Tractors do many jobs, including pulling other machines, like ploughs.

They have big, thick wheels for grip in muddy fields.

Tractor

A plough is used to loosen and turn soil before crops are planted.

Blades on the plough dig into the soil.

Plough

Combine harvesters are used to cut and harvest crops.

Sharp blades cut the crops, while spinning spikes pull them into the machine.

Combine Harvester

This machine is attached to the back of a tractor to plant potatoes.

It drops potatoes into the ground and covers them over with soil.

Potato Planter

This machine is used to milk a cow.

These tubes are attached to a cow's udders to pump milk into a big container.

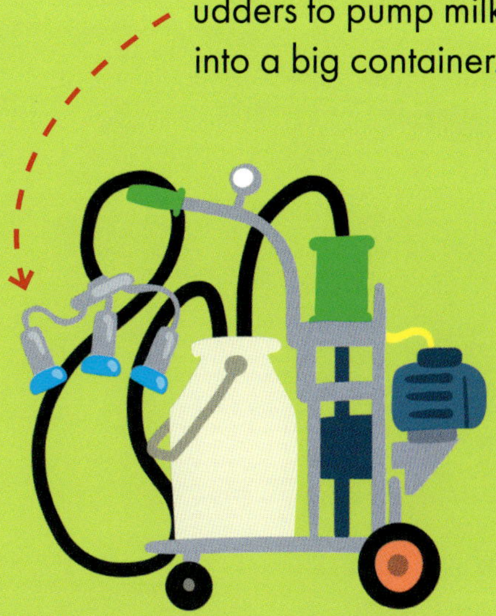

Milking Machine

A baler packs cut hay into bales so that it can be easily transported and stored.

Once the machine has made a bale, it drops it out of the back.

Hay Baler

AT THE AUTO-REPAIR SHOP

Mechanics have lots of special tools and machines to fix cars and other vehicles.

AT THE AUTO-REPAIR SHOP

An engine hoist is used to lift a heavy **engine** out of a car.

Pumping this lever moves the arm up or down.

Engine Hoist

This lifts a vehicle off the ground so mechanics can get underneath to work on it.

Vehicle Lift

These controls move the lift up and down.

This machine checks a wheel is balanced, so that it spins smoothly.

A wheel is attached here, and the machine spins it round.

Wheel Balancer

An oil drainer is used to remove old oil from a vehicle, so that it can be replaced.

The old oil collects in this tank.

Oil Drainer

This machine can recharge or kickstart a car battery.

These clips are used to attach the battery to the machine.

Battery Charger

A spray gun is used to give cars a new coat of paint.

When the trigger is pulled, the machine sprays paint evenly onto the car.

Spray Gun

AT A ROADWORKS SITE

Have you ever thought about how roads get made? It takes a lot of machines.

AT A ROADWORKS SITE

Graders are used to flatten out the ground before the new road surface is put down.

Road Grader

A paver spreads a layer of **asphalt** onto the ground to make a new road surface.

Road Paver

A road roller is used to flatten down the new asphalt.

Road Roller

A milling machine removes old road surfaces, so that they can be replaced.

Old asphalt is chewed up and pushed out through this **conveyor belt** arm.

Milling Machine

Also called a jackhammer, this drill breaks through hard surfaces, like concrete.

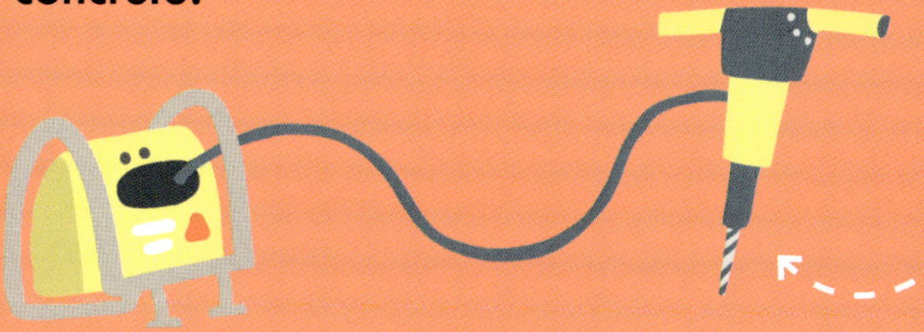

It moves up and down very fast and hammers the ground hard to break it up.

Pneumatic Drill

This is used to paint road markings on a new road.

Paint comes out here as the machine is pushed along, leaving a smooth line.

Road Marking Machine

FIND AND SEEK!

Can you find which machine each of these pictures are a part of?

1.

CLUE: This machine turns the wheel round to test that it spins smoothly.

2.

CLUE: This machine is used to flatten down the asphalt on roads.

3.

CLUE: This machine attaches to a cow's udders to pump out milk.

4.

CLUE: This machine is used to clear the ground to get it ready for building.

5.

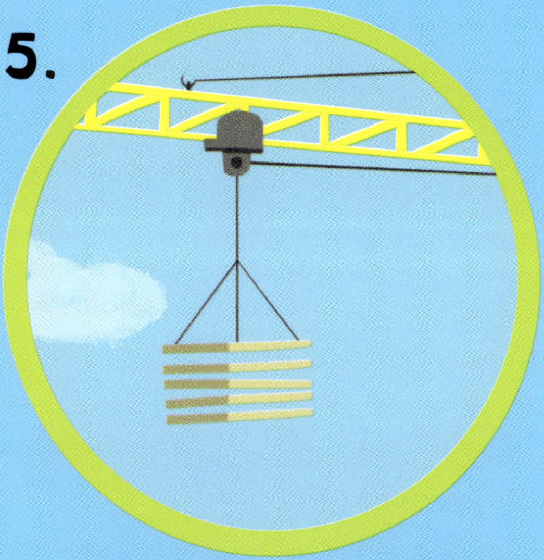

CLUE: This machine is used to lift large and heavy objects.

6.

CLUE: This machine spreads asphalt onto the ground to make a new road surface.

7.

CLUE: This machine plants a particular vegetable on the farm.

8.

CLUE: This machine collects old oil from a car.

DID YOU FIND THEM ALL?

Answers can be found on page 24.

GLOSSARY

Asphalt
A material used to make smooth road surfaces.

Bales
A large bundle of something, such as hay.

Conveyor belt
A moving surface used to transport objects from one place to another.

Engine
Part of a machine or vehicle that turns fuel into energy to make it move.

Hydraulic
Something that is moved by a liquid, such as water, being put under pressure.

Mechanics
A person whose job it is to repair and look after vehicles and machines.

Road markings
Lines, symbols or words painted on roads to give drivers important information.

FIND AND SEEK ANSWERS

ANSWERS: 1. Wheel Balancer, 2. Road Roller, 3. Milking Machine, 4. Bulldozer, 5. Crane, 6. Road Paver, 7. Potato Planter, 8. Oil Drainer.